essentials

essentials provide up-to-date knowledge in a concentrated form. The essence of what matters as "state of the art" in the current professional discussion or in practice. *essentials* inform quickly, uncomplicatedly and comprehensibly

- as an introduction to a current topic from your field of expertise
- as an introduction to a subject area that is still unknown to you
- as an insight, in order to be able to speak on the subject

The books in electronic and printed form present the expert knowledge of Springer specialist authors in a compact form. They are particularly suitable for use as eBooks on tablet PCs, eBook readers and smartphones. *essentials:* Knowledge modules from economics, social sciences and the humanities, from technology and the natural sciences, as well as from medicine, psychology and the health professions. From renowned authors of all Springer publishing brands.

Volker Völzke

Patients with Memory Disorders

An Introduction for Psychotherapists

 Springer

Volker Völzke
Leitung Therapie, Psychologie and Neuropsychologie
VAMED Klinik Hattingen
Hattingen, Germany

ISSN 2197-6708   ISSN 2197-6716   (electronic)
ISBN 978-3-658-39799-9   ISBN 978-3-658-39800-2   (eBook)
https://doi.org/10.1007/978-3-658-39800-2

Preface

In training courses for psychotherapists in particular, but also for other groups, one question is asked again and again: What can I do with patients with cognitive impairment and specifically learning and memory disorders? How do I modify my therapy so that it works?

Psychotherapists report: "Actually, I would like to offer cognitive behavioural therapy or analytical therapy, but the person concerned keeps forgetting aspects discussed and the homework. It is not uncommon for the therapist or the affected person to break off the therapy. I don't like to take such patients because I can't assess some aspects at all."

What assessment and what tools are available and what do memory deficits mean for therapy and counselling? Can I even do psychotherapy with people with memory disorders? On the other hand, there are also more and more people in psychotherapy who care for relatives. How can I support and advise them in a professionally qualified way? In the work with affected persons, it becomes clear how central our memory is. The *essential* wants to give practice-oriented answers to these urgent questions.

Hattingen, Germany   Volker Völzke

Acknowledgements

I would like to thank my university teachers Prof. Dr. G. Ettlinger (University of Bielefeld) and Prof. Dr. W. Hartje (RWTH Aachen) and my clinical chief physicians Prof. Dr. W. Ischebeck and Dr. A. Petershofer (Hattingen) and of course all former and current colleagues of all disciplines for many years of inspiration, motivation, support and appreciation. I thank Dr. Petershofer, PD Dr. Sparing, Mrs. Römer, Mrs. Lindgraf and many colleagues for helpful comments and correction of the manuscript. My special appreciation goes to the many concerned people who accompanied me from civilian service to clinical work.

What You Can Find in This *Essential*

- Information on how learning and memory work
- A study of the Information on areas in the brain where learning and memory are represented
- Clearly described clinical pictures that reveal cause memory disorders
- Concrete instructions on how to diagnose and treat the disorders
- Practical recommendations on how to implement psychotherapy with affected persons

Contents

Introduction

1

Memory and **learning** or remembering belong together and interact in everyday life. Learning refers to the acquisition of knowledge and skills, remembering to the recall of factual knowledge or episodes (retrospective), but also to things to be done (prospective). Remembering is not a retrieval from a "hard disk", but a constantly new "re-constructive" process. The retrieval itself changes the content and is relatively easy to manipulate even in healthy people.

Furthermore, the **recognition** of places, faces or objects is part of our everyday life. Without this skill, we would not be able to find paths again or identify people in a group. Social interaction would be completely different without memory.

Therefore, learning and memory are also listed in the International Classification of Functions and Disabilities (ICF) of the WHO as an important aspect of body functions, participation and activity. Environmental factors (e.g. family support, occupational affiliation) and person-related factors (e.g. individual processing mechanisms of experiences and illnesses, previous mental illnesses) represent positive or negative variables influencing memory performance (see Fig. 1.1).

Learning and memory (Hildebrandt, 2019; Kolb & Whishaw, 2021) are based on neuronal processes in the central nervous system. The center is the brain, which weighs about 1.5 kg, with the brain surface (cortex; Figs. 1.2 and 1.3) and underlying structures. The cortex is divided into 4 brain lobes (lobi). Additionally there are the cerebellum and subcortical structures and a transition to the spinal cord. However, learning processes probably also take place in other regions of the body (e.g. including the autonomic nervous system in the abdominal brain).

Certain functions are assigned to the cortical lobes (lat. Lobi), subcortical structures and the cerebellum (see Table 1.1). This assignment is based on patient

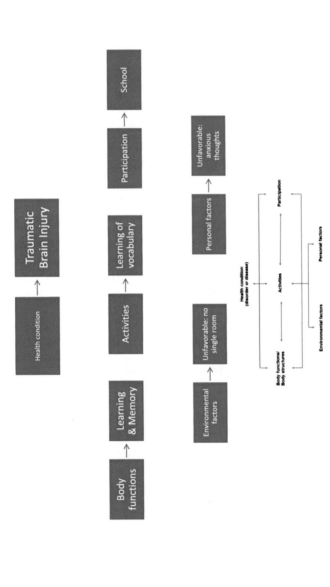

Fig. 1.1 Implementation of the ICF model in memory disorders

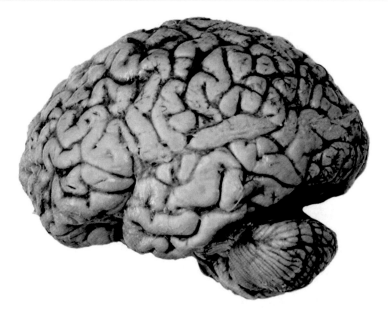

Fig. 1.2 Lateral view of the human brain from the left. The meninges are partially removed due to dissection. (Source: Huggenberger et al., 2019)

studies with brain injuries (lesions) and on results of functional imaging (including functional magnetic resonance imaging "fMRI").

For adequate functioning the brain needs oxygen and nutrients, which are transported to the brain via the bloodstream. Therefore, disturbances of the blood supply (see below) are extremely important for the development of learning and memory disorders and other disturbances. The blood supply to the brain is provided by four arteries (see Fig. 1.4), which are organized in pairs (carotid and vertebral arteries, respectively). The arteria (tributaries) are connected to each other in a ring at the base of the brain (Circulus Willisii). This anatomical arrangement limits the effects of individual occlusions.

Learning and memory are based on neuronal principles and depend on an adequate blood and oxygen supply

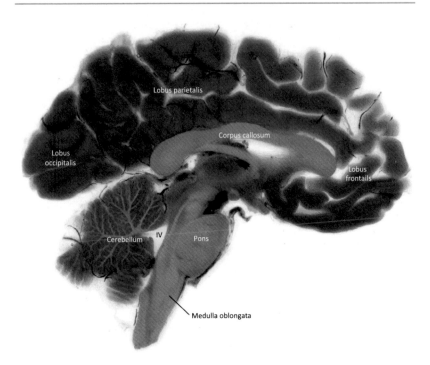

Fig. 1.3 Lateral plastination preparation of the human brain. (Source: Huggenberger et al., 2019)

Table 1.1 Functional areas and assignment to brain areas (simplified)

Areas and common designations	Left	Right
Frontal lobe, lobus frontalis	Language, behavioural control, executive incl. learning strategy, speaking, working memory	Behavioural control, executive incl. learning strategy, speaking, awareness system
Parietal lobe, lobus parietalis	Speech comprehension, spatial orientation, awareness system	Spatial orientation, awareness system
Temporal lobe, lobus temporalis	Naming, linguistic memory	Spatial orientation, figural memory
Occipital lobe, lobus occipitalis	Vision (right visual field)	Vision (left visual field)
Cerebellum	Motor coordination, speech, executive functions, movement learning	Motor coordination, speech, executive functions, movement learning

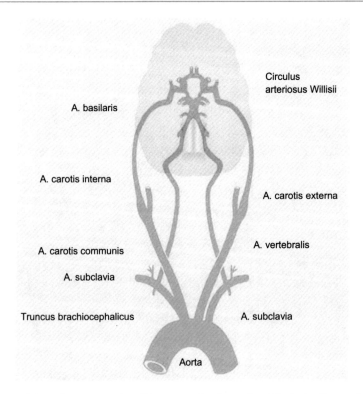

Fig. 1.4 Schematic representation of the aorta and main arteries of the brain. (Source: **Peter Ringleb, Roland Veltkamp, Stefan Schwab, Martin Bendszus, p. 184,** in Hacke, 2016)

References

Hacke, W. (2016). *Neurologie* (14. Aufl.). Springer.
Hildebrandt, H. (2019). *Cognitive rehabilitation of memory*. Academic.
Huggenberger, S., Moser, N., Schröder, H., Cozzi, B., Granato, A., & Merighi, A. (2019). *Neuroanatomie des Menschen*. Springer.
Kolb, B., & Wishaw, I. (2021). *Fundamentals of human neuropsychology* (8th ed.). Worth.

Memory Functions and Systems

2

In the different systems of general psychology, bio- or neuropsychology (e.g. Hildebrandt, 2019; Winson et al., 2017), essential elements of memory and learning are defined and specified. Distinctions are made in the established three-component model (see Table 2.1) between the temporal dimensions of ultra-short-term, short-term, and long-term memory. Working memory is often mentioned as a supplement.

On the one hand, working memory is assigned to short-term memory, but on the other hand it is often assigned to the executive functional areas (e.g. planning & problem solving). In the working memory, verbal or figural information (material specificity) is held and manipulated (focusing the cognitive capacities on one area, e.g. in reading and arithmetic).

The other memory components differ in duration, capacity and significance. Simplified, different neurotransmitters (including dopamine) trigger electro-chemical stimulus transmission. The information to be learned goes through a temporal process.

Material specifics include **procedural** learning (e.g. movements), **figural** learning (e.g. places, drawings), **verbal** learning (e.g. words for…) and **episodic** learning (e.g. remembering events, source memory).

A special form of learning is **priming.** Memory information is activated by an emerging stimulus (e.g. words, images, sounds) so that subsequent information can be recognized and processed more quickly. This enables to assess situations more quickly. A readiness, unconscious expectation or alertness is generated. The basis are the primary sensory areas (vision, hearing, sensing) in the cortex. They are prepared by "learning" for similar situations in the future.

Table 2.1 Memory functions, components and properties

Area	Duration	Capacity	Basics and processes	Meaning
Ultra-short-term memory/ sensory memory; iconic memory, sensory register	Milliseconds	High	Sense organs	Immediate decisions
Short-term memory	Seconds to minutes	7 ± 2 units	Excitation circuits; alteration of synaptic transmission	Decisions
Working memory	Seconds to minutes	Limited (see above)	Excitatory circuits in frontal and parietal areas; phonological loop on the left, visual spatial notepad on the right, connection to long-term memory by means of episodic buffer, role of the central executive	"Editing" information & manipulation; keeps information "online"
Long-term memory "library"	Information that is retained for more than a few minutes; lifetime information	"Unlimited"	Anatomical changes especially in the hippocampus & cortex	Knowledge retrieval (explicit, partly also implicit), episodes (Where did what happen?) and skills (implicit)

Often a distinction is made between **explicit** and **implicit** learning and memory processes (see Table 2.2). The former is simplified "conscious" while implicit learning is rather "unconscious". We do not even notice that we are learning, especially in social situations with intensive interaction. Explicit sometimes means **declarative** and involves "knowledge". This knowledge can be verbalized. Implicit also means non-declarative, refers to "skill" and is less amenable to verbalization (including emotional learning). Our memory information is remembered or recognized freely, in part after cueing stimuli.

Long-term memory enables to recognise people, places and objects in everyday life, even in the face of change, and includes the temporal classification of

Table 2.2 Principles of learning psychology

Learn	Process	Importance in everyday life
Habituation	An automatic reaction does not take place in case of repetition	Reduction of anxiety; habituation (reduced reaction) to drafts, noise, light
Sensitizing, "becoming more sensitive"	An automatic reaction takes place even faster or earlier	Anxiety; increased response to an external stimulus (e.g. sound, image, draft)
Classical conditioning	An originally neutral stimulus becomes a trigger stimulus by coupling	A stimulus takes on a new meaning; emergence of fears
Instrumental conditioning	Learning through success/ reward or punishment	Multiple behaviours (avoidance) and cognitions
Model learning	Learning through observation or imitation	Multiple behaviors and cognitions (attitudes)
Learning by doing	Improvement of the storage	School learning, repeated experiences
Learning by improving the depth of processing	Improvement of the storage	Learning at school, study and work
Learning through strategy	Improvement of the storage	Learning at school, study and work

episodes (What came first?) or locations of episodes (anatomically relevant is the praecunaeus).

Learning processes (see Table 2.2) include habituation, classical conditioning, instrumental conditioning and learning from a model. Furthermore, there is **procedural** learning and a corresponding memory. The example of riding a bicycle or opening a bottle with a screw cap is striking. Once learned, we can usually recall this skill without further thought.

In part, these processes are learned or improved through **observation** (e.g. movement sequences in sports). Apraxia (disturbance of action retrieval after brain damage) can be interpreted as a disturbance in the retrieval of procedural information. The anatomical basis for movement is the prefrontal cortex for intention and in the motor cortex, basal ganglia and cerebellum for procedural learning. Especially in procedural learning, repetition plays an important role in optimizing movements (e.g. serving in tennis).

The **body memory** also enables us to remember and imagine sensations (e.g. touches). Pathologically, however, it also leads to "phantom pain" after amputations or to other forms of pain that exist ("pain memory") without the original trigger. In addition to cortical and subcortical processes, physiological changes in the spinal cord level are involved.

Table 2.3 Forgetting and related processes

Process	Foundation	Meaning
Track decay	Biochemical process	Loss of knowledge ("last in, first out")
Retroactive interference	What is learned later interferes with what was learned earlier	School and vocational learning
Proactive interference	Earlier learning interferes with later learning	School and vocational learning
Forgetting curve	Strong forgetting at an early stage after the learning process	School and vocational learning
So-called "permastore" (analogy of the thawing earth)	Biochemical process	Loss of knowledge ("last in, first out")
False memories	Remembering is always a re-constructive process and prone to disruption	Remembering episodes (misattribution)
See above	Manipulation by alternative content and distortion by current attitudes, evaluations and feelings	Remembering episodes

Habits and **routines** (e.g. wallet in the top drawer) help us cope in everyday life, "save" cognitive resources, so that we do not have to remember, evaluate and decide every time. Ultimately, addictions are also products of learning and habit formation and are established through reward, immediate stress reduction and physiological change.

Prospective memory enables us to successfully manage things in the future (at a specific point in time). Striking examples are changing car tyres in spring and autumn or remembering materials (e.g. papers, presentations) at work.

Forgetting things to do (e.g. homework, shopping) is probably what we often mean when we say we are "forgetful" (Table 2.3).

Forgetting can help in everyday life by eliminating unpleasant experiences (e.g. disputes) from our current memory. Forgetting reduces stress on the memory system.

> Learning, memory and forgetting can be differentiated into different processes and structures.

References

Hildebrandt, H. (2019). *Cognitive rehabilitation of memory*. Academic Press.
Winson, R., Wilson, B., & Bateman, A. (2017). *The Brain Injury Rehabilitation Workbook*. New York: Guilford Press.

Learning and Memory as a Temporal Process

3

Initially, the **sensory organs** transmit information to the primary **information centers** in the brain. For vision the information is transported to the thalami (lat. corpi geniculatum laterali) and after switching to the **occipital lobes** (see above). For hearing, after passing the area of the thalami, the so-called **Heschl's Area** (lat. gyri temporales transversi; area 41) in the depth of the temporal lobe is responsible. These in turn pass them on to the cortex and special centers (also subcortical).

In parallel, this information is evaluated in terms of relevance and emotional significance. Information that is not perceived with sufficient intensity cannot be retained. At the very beginning of the process, our **interests** and **curiosity** and related **attentional aspects** play an important role. Alertness, vigilance, selective, divided and spatial attention limit our cognitive capacity in learning (similar to a bottleneck). This information is structured intentionally or automatically, associated linked (i.e. with what is known or similar), usually verbalized or visualized.

3.1   Neuroanatomical Foundations of Learning and Memory

The **sensory organs** are the initial instances of learning (see above). So their injury limits learning. Hearing disorders, for example, often lead to apparent cognitive deficits, but are also a risk factor for the development of cognitive deficits through lack of stimulation and caused isolation.

The **thalamus** or thalami are paired and are switching stations for information from the sensory organs to the cortex. Injuries often occur after infarctions or cerebral hemorrhages.

The **basal ganglia** are also paired and are located subcortically. They include the caudate (often activating) putamen and the pallidum. The putamen and the pallidum are collectively called the striatum. The substantia nigra is also assigned to the striatum (often inhibitory). These nuclei and structures are separated from each other by fibrous masses (capsula interna). The basal area plays an important role in all learning processes and also in many motor processes. The basal ganglia often suffer damage in the course of infarctions. Furthermore, they can be affected by degenerative processes (including dopamine deficiency).

The **cerebellum** is an important component of motor and procedural learning. Damages are caused by strokes, but also in degenerative processes. Furthermore, the cerebellar areas are part of a network that processes executive tasks and speech.

The **hippocampi** (similar to a recumbent seahorse) are centrally paired. Probably all learning processes run via the hippocampi. Lesions of this structure lead to severe learning and memory disorders. The significance of this area is seen after operations in this area (including epilepsy surgery), in cerebral hypoxia and in inflammatory processes (encephalitis).

The **cortex** with its different areas stores knowledge and episodic information. Injuries of the cortex can occur after various diseases (e.g. traumas, infarctions, operations, degeneration). In particular, injuries in the **temporal brain** cause memory deficits, while injuries in the frontal brain cause secondary memory deficits (insufficient attention and strategy).

Explicit memory is often associated with the basal **forebrain** (lat. nucleus basalis), a part of the frontal brain. The **limbic** system is responsible for emotional aspects of learning and memory. The "**Papez circle**" (concept about the connection of hippocampus, mamillary body, gyrus cinguli) or the **fronto-thalamic circle** are further cortical or subcortical structures that are extremely important for learning and memory.

The left "Papez circuit" is responsible for the storage of episodes and facts, while the right one enables the storage of spatial states (including the spatial relationship of objects to each other). **Conduction pathways,** such as the "Tractus uncinatus", which connects the basal forebrain with the temporal brain, are injured in subarachnoid hemorrhages from the arteria communicans anterior (so-called "AcoA syndrome").

Learning and memory can be temporally differentiated and neuroanatomically assigned.

Learning and Memory Over the Lifespan

4

Developmental psychology knows sensitive phases (characterized by maturation processes, among other things) and **developmental tasks or milestones** for all ages up to old age. The developmental milestones (including learning to calculate and write, living together as a couple) include cognitive-affective and social developmental steps (e.g. Forsyth & Newton, 2018) (Table 4.1).

Adults cannot remember episodes of early childhood later (**"infantile amnesia"**). The not yet completed brain maturation (hippocampus-fornix connection) is probably the cause. Memories often begin in "Kindergarten", or only very significant episodes are remembered. However, the memories are extremely susceptible to **distortion** (reconstruction).

Especially in children and adolescents with acquired brain damage, the **developmental milestones or tasks** that actually exist are not mastered or are mastered with a significant time delay. In developmental neuropsychology, this phenomenon is referred to as **"growing into the deficit"**. The myth of the significantly more plastic infant brain is thus clearly put into perspective. In concrete terms, it means that shortly after an accident (or similar event) there may still be just about average performance in learning and memory (or in other cognitive areas), but after a few years there is an important performance deficit. Learning and memory disorders accompany children and adolescents in particular over a period of decades. The affected persons and their family do not have any experience in unimpaired development.

> Learning and memory skills develop over the lifespan and deficits lead to different effects. The effects are often chronic.

© The Author(s), under exclusive license to Springer Fachmedien Wiesbaden GmbH, part of Springer Nature 2023
V. Völzke, *Patients with Memory Disorders*, essentials,
https://doi.org/10.1007/978-3-658-39800-2_4

Table 4.1 Learning and memory across the lifespan (simplified)

Age range	Learning and development	Research methods and assessment	Importance of learning and memory disorders for participation
Babies and toddlers	Multimodal; non-declarative memory exist; remembering for days	Experimental (duration of fixation, e.g.) and developmental scales; wide variability in development	Developmental delay; living in the nuclear family; early intervention
Toddler and preschool age	Multimodal (incl. language); autobiographical memory; good recognition from the age of 4; memory span with 3–4 items	Developmental scales and tests; wide variability in development	Developmental delay; living in the nuclear family; early intervention
Primary school age	Cultural techniques, social behaviours (sitting still, working in a group, e.g.); memory span 4–6 items; verbal and figural learning improve	Developmental tests with memory tasks; high variability of development; school tests; special memory tests (including VLMT)	Schooling: Inclusion or special school; disadvantage compensation; living in the nuclear family
Adolescence	Establishment of cultural techniques; social behaviour (including relationships); reflection on biographical memories	Special memory tests (including VLMT)	Schooling: Inclusion or special school; disadvantage compensation; living in nuclear family; change of perspectives; development of autonomy questionable
Young adulthood	Graduation and career choice; relationships	Special memory tests	Promotion, compensation for disadvantages; finding and testing a profession; clarification of living situation (groups, family); further development of autonomy questionable
Adulthood	Work and family	Special memory tests	Career search and testing; clarification of the living situation (groups, family)
Higher adulthood	Work and family; retirement planning	Special memory tests	Clarification of career prospects; life situation
High age	Retirement and old age	Special memory tests	Clarification of life perspective (home, family)

Reference

Forsyth, R., & Newton, R. (2018). *Oxford specialist handbooks in paediatrics – Paediatric neurology*. University Press.

Negative Factors Due to Learning and Memory

In everyday life, a variety of factors can negatively influence learning and memory performance. They must be considered in our daily work.

Checklist 1: Factors Influencing Learning and Memory

- **Fluid deficiency** (reduced oxygen supply via the blood flow; chronic fluid deficiency favours the development of cognitive deficits)
- **Pain** (lower cognitive resources; distraction; concomitant effects of **pain** medications).
- **Blood sugar fluctuations**
- **Infections** (weakened people have low reserve capacities; concomitant effect of antibiotics)
- **Medications** (e.g. blood pressure medications, beta-blockers, all psychotropic medications [including diazepam], antiepileptic medications).
- **Delirium** (alcohol withdrawal delirium, postoperative cognitive dysfunction "POCD" up to 4 days)
- **Multiple surgeries** (risk in patients >60 years, with lower educational level [lower reserve capacity], pain patients, spine/heart surgeries, identification of patients at risk).
- **Lung diseases** (including COPD "chronic obstructive pulmonary disease"; risk: severity of COPD).
- Chronic or acute **poisoning** (see below)

© The Author(s), under exclusive license to Springer Fachmedien Wiesbaden GmbH, part of Springer Nature 2023
V. Völzke, *Patients with Memory Disorders*, essentials,
https://doi.org/10.1007/978-3-658-39800-2_5

5.1   Mental Disorders

Cognitive disorders are common in the context of mental disorders (e.g. Trapp et al., 2022; Thoma et al., 2013). This is partly based on changes in **neurotransmitters** and **psychological factors** that alter learning and memory (so-called **moderator variables**). These include insufficient effort, distorted expectations and frequently dysfunctional working styles.

5.2   Learning and Memory Disorders or Suspected Dementia in Depression

In the context of acute **depressive episodes** and chronic **depression** (often older sufferers), moderate impairments in learning ability are evident. Psychological assessments reveal disturbances especially in delayed recall and delayed recognition, but also a reduced learning curve and disturbances due to interference (mutual inhibition of information). Especially unstructured material is learned particularly poorly. In everyday life, patients benefit from structure and learning strategies. Memory spans and simple working memory (repeating numbers backwards) are sometimes hardly impaired.

Clinically, the question of differentiating between dementia and depression (pseudodementia) arises. In the case of **pseudodementia**, the affected persons are usually younger, complain more about the deficits, and are otherwise rather adynamic and reserved in their behaviour, show feelings of guilt, often a circadian disturbance (morning) and fear of failure. Furthermore, it is highly relevant that the self-assessment of those patients with pseudodementia is usually significantly worse than the real test performance. Furthermore, the initiation of the examination (visit to the doctor, testing) in „real "dementia patients usually comes from the relatives and only in a few cases from the affected person. Dementia patients usually show an unawareness of the deficits.

A chronic change in mood (e.g. sadness) leads to a deterioration in learning and memory performance later in life, especially in higher age.

5.3   Learning and Memory Impairment in Psychosis

In acute phases, all cognitive processes are severely impaired. The main areas affected are verbal learning and declarative memory. Presumably, dysregulation processes in the dopaminergic system are relevant. In chronic phases, deficits due to further changes in the system of neurotransmitters and deficits due to neuroleptic medication become apparent. Depending on the chronicity of the psychosis, the learning and memory deficits are more or less reversible (Trapp et al., 2022).

5.4   Learning and Memory Disorders in Anorexia (Lat. Anorexia Nervosa)

In the context of severe anorexia, massive and partly non-reversible learning and memory disorders may occur. Due to the electrolyte changes that occur because of pathological eating behaviour, there are disturbances in neurotransmitter production (noradrenaline and serotonin) and changes in brain morphology.

5.5   Learning and Memory Disorders Associated with THC Use

The high concentration of THC in cannabis plants leads to stronger acute effects (e.g. hallucinations) but also to long-lasting cognitive disorders (including working memory). Children and adolescents are particularly at risk.

> Learning and memory deficits exist as a consequence of physiological disorders and in the context of psychological disorders (physiological changes and moderator variables).

References

Thoma, P., Friedmann, C., & Suchan, B. (2013). Empathy and social problem solving in alcohol dependence, mood disorders and selected personality disorders. *Neuroscience and Biobehavioral Reviews, 37*(2013), 448–470.

Trapp, W., Heid, A., Röder, S., Wimmer, F., & Hajak, G. (2022). Cognitive remediation in psychiatric disorders: State of the evidence, future perspectives, and some bold ideas. *Brain Sciences, 12*, 683. https://doi.org/10.3390/brainsci12060683

Acquired Brain Damage

6

Moderate and severe learning and memory disorders usually result from acquired brain damage (see below) or from degenerative processes (see Chap. 7. Dementia).

Stroke

After occlusion of a cerebral artery **(syn. insult, infarction, stroke),** the downstream supply areas die (see Table 6.1). The faster the medical or mechanical recanalization of the vessel, the better the outcome ("time is brain"). A stroke can affect all neuroanatomical structures, which are relevant for learning and memory. One component of therapy and rehabilitation is **secondary prophylaxis** with education on necessary **behavioural changes** (diet, sport, stress, etc.) and **medication.**

6.1 Subarachnoid Hemorrhage (SAB)

Caused by trauma, but more frequently in the context of **a ruptured aneurysm** (presumably congenital vascular outpouching), blood flows into the subarachnoid space (meninges from the outside to the inside: dura mater, pia mater, arachnoid mater) and so destroys and displaces brain tissue. Often, blood in the subarachnoid space also causes vasospasms (i.e. spasmodic constriction of the vessels), which additionally limit the function of the brain and can lead to an infarction. Increased intracranial pressure causes further damage.

© The Author(s), under exclusive license to Springer Fachmedien
Wiesbaden GmbH, part of Springer Nature 2023
V. Völzke, *Patients with Memory Disorders*, essentials,
https://doi.org/10.1007/978-3-658-39800-2_6

Table 6.1 Neuropsychological disorders according to vascular syndromes (focus on learning and memory disorders)

Vascular Region	Neuropsychology
Left middle cerebral artery	Aphasia (speech comprehension and production; communication disorder)
	Alexia (inability to read)
	Agraphia (inability to write)
	Language-related learning and memory disorders
Right middle cerebral artery	Spatial orientation disorders and figural-spatial memory disorders
	Often anosognosia (not perceiving one's own illness)
Left anterior cerebral artery	Personality changes with impulsive behaviour and further planning disorders (executive dysfunction)
	Attention disorders (selective and divided attention)
	Disorders of verbal learning and word retrieval
Right anterior	Anosognosia (see above)
	Disturbance of attention (selective and divided attention)
Cerebral artery	Personality changes with impulsive and disorganized behaviour & perseverative tendencies (see concomitant executive disorders)
	Disturbance of spatial and figural learning

6.2   Intracerebral Hemorrhage (ICB)

Blood flows ("bloody stroke") into the brain tissue, destroys, and displaces it. The cause is often traumatic. Internal diseases (e.g. high blood pressure; in the context of oncological diseases, partly due to vascular malformations), can also cause hemorrhage.

Practical Example

A merchant suffers a left truncal ganglion hemorrhage with ventricular herniation. He exhibits a severe amnestic syndrome and a mild speech disorder. The short story of the RBMT (see below) cannot be reproduced. After rehabilitation, we observed an increase from 0 to 4 correct remembered items. The VLMT (see below) shows no learning curve (2, 3, 5, 3, 3 correct items). After discharge, the affected person benefits from clear structures and can use his smartphone with massive support. Relatives send information and instructions for action. First memories of episodes show up. Furthermore, independent walking with the dog is possible (identical routes) and it is possible to stay at home alone for half days. ◄

The examination of patients with **aphasia** (acquired disorder of fully learned language; mostly left-brain lesion) is a special challenge. A prerequisite for a differential examination is the testing of verbal language comprehension. One of the tests available for this purpose is the **Token Test**. Instructions are given in ascending complexity and implementation is assessed (e.g. "Show me a green piece; Place the blue circle next to the green triangle; First touch the small yellow circle and then the large blue square"). Very simplistically, sentence completion tasks can also be performed to assess verbal language comprehension (e.g. If you are hungry, buy yourself something to…). In aphasics, reading comprehension is often impaired as well. Non-verbal procedures (e.g. recall of the Rey-Figure) are also available for the test-psychological investigation of learning and memory.

6.3   Brain Tumour (Incl. Chemobrain and Radiation)

The localization determines the symptoms. Learning and memory disorders are frequently seen in tumours in the area of the frontal brain (often sphenoid meningiomas), but also in tumours affecting the hormonal axis (including pituitary adenomas). Malignant tumours (including grade IV astrocytomas and glioblastomas) with infiltration of large areas of the brain usually also cause important learning and memory impairments. These and gradual personality changes are often an early symptom of the disease.

Radiation and **chemotherapy** further lead to additive and rather unspecific cognitive impairments (so-called "Chemobrain"). In addition to the direct effects of cytostatic drugs on the hippocampus, associated sleep disorders, hormonal changes, psychological stress and other factors play an important role. After cessation of chemotherapy, the disorders sometimes show chronicity. Patients at risk are multimorbid elderly or very debilitated persons. These aspects should definitely be taken into account in oncological and especially psycho-oncological therapy.

6.4   Memory Impairment After Other Brain Surgeries

The localization of the lesions determines the symptoms. **Epilepsy surgery** with the aim of reducing seizures in the area of the hippocampus often leads to acute, but also stable i.e. chronic learning and memory deficits. Other surgical indications are vascular malformations (e.g. angiomas).

6.5   Traumatic Brain Injury (TBI)

Traumatic brain injuries are typical causes of learning and memory disorders in childhood, adolescence and young adulthood. The accident mechanisms partly change over the lifespan (e.g. accidents in road traffic as pedestrian or cyclist, sports accidents, accidents in the household).

On the one hand, the localization of the injury (point of impact **"coup"**; actively against an obstacle or passively through a moving object) determines the symptoms. On the other hand, there are **"Contre-Coup-Phenomena"** (opposite the point of impact) and **shear forces** that act on the brain and cause micro lesions or changes in brain metabolism. Deficits in learning and memory are very common in severe traumatic brain injuries (severity I to IV). A distinction is made between **open** (with skull fracture) and **closed** craniocerebral trauma. Especially in the early phase of rehabilitation, these are often not sufficiently visible and not taken into account, because they are hidden by the general weakness and low dynamics of the affected person.

Even in cases of **mild TBI** (grade I or concussion; often in the household or during sports), rest of at least 1 week (also reduction of the use of electronic devices) is recommended. Just a few sufferers report and show symptoms beyond the one-year period. Frequent minor accidents have an additive effect. The therapeutic attitude is determined by a positive prognosis.

Furthermore, depending on the accident mechanism and degree of severity, affected persons may also experience **adjustment disorders** and, in severe cases, **post-traumatic stress disorders** (PTSD). Serious accidents with entrapment, death of strangers or relatives or crimes could trigger these and lead additively to cognitive disorders. During psychotherapy, it is necessary to consider the cognitive disorders. In some cases, these patients have no memory of the accident itself and therefore no stressful memories ("flashbacks"). Therapy in intensive care or early rehabilitation can also lead to psychological stress effects (e.g. experience of helplessness, loss of intimacy). Children and adolescents in particular show inconsistent and rather diffuse symptoms of the stress reaction (e.g. restlessness, anger).

Practical Example

A young woman suffers from a severe traffic accident with Politrauma as a passenger. In addition to multiple fractures and attention deficits caused by the head injury, there are also clear deficits in working memory (backwards number recitation, and verbal learning and memory of the VLMT). Independent living is no longer successful after inpatient rehabilitation and the affected person moves back to her parents. Goals include the development of individual private and, if necessary, professional perspectives and compensation of the memory deficits through external help.

A high school student suffers from a severe car accident with Politrauma including TBI. After inpatient rehabilitation, gradual reintegration into school takes place. With maximum support from the family and the school, reintegration succeeds. Despite very good improvements, there are still deficits in the delayed retention of information (VLMT). In everyday life, especially the learning of vocabulary and the learning of facts require a lot of time. The child needs sufficient recovery phases. ◄

6.6   Cerebral Hypoxia/Anoxia (Including Resuscitation)

Oxygen undersupply over a longer period leads to diffuse damage of the brain. Memory-relevant structures (hippocampus, mammillary body, etc.) and the cerebellum seem to be particularly sensitive to this undersupply (>3 min). Patients have an **unfavourable prognosis** especially in learning and memory performance. Long-term inpatient care and lifelong need for support is a common consequence.

An untreated **sleep apnea syndrome** can cause slow developing learning and memory deficits.

Infantile cerebral palsy (ICP) represents a special form of hypoxia. Pre-, peri- or postnatal, there are disturbances in the oxygen supply to the infant's brain and can cause severe disorders. These affect not only the motor function but also the cognitive areas including learning and memory. Some of those affected have a chronic mental handicap. They are dependent on early support/therapy and then need lifelong support.

Practical Example

A technician suffers from a cardiac arrest and is resuscitated. In the cardiological rehabilitation cognitive deficits are noticed but not diagnosed. There were no cardiac problems during the occupational reintegration. The patient himself retrospectively had no awareness of deficit in everyday life (e.g. forgotten appointments and arrangements). In the course of his professional activity, he made several significant mistakes and was dismissed because of his memory disorders. A depression is also clarified as a differential diagnosis (see below). The assessment reveals severe deficits in the VLMT (learning curve) and in areas of working memory. ◄

6.7   Encephalitis and Meningitis

In particular, **viral encephalitis,** often caused by a **herpes virus,** damages memory-sensitive structures. Depending on the diagnosis and the timing of the effective medication, mild to severe disturbances in learning and memory may be observed. Furthermore, there are also infections of the brain caused by bacteria or worms (e.g. neurolues), which can trigger severe cognitive disorders if they remain untreated.

A special form, which only occurred a few years ago but is increasing in frequency, is **Anti-NMDA Receptor Encephalitis** (autoimmune disease in which the body develops antibodies against the NMDA receptors), which can also cause severe deficits (e.g. memory, personality changes). Antibodies block signal transmission in the brain. The hippocampal regions are often affected. Triggers of the autoimmune disease are infections or paraneoplastic processes. New drug approaches (including cytostatic) seem to improve the prognosis.

Meningitis is an inflammation of the meninges caused by bacteria and, more rarely, viruses and leads to immediate severe deficits (including learning and memory). Improved diagnostic and therapeutic options have significantly improved the prognosis. If untreated, about half of those affected die from cerebral edema or sepsis. Early therapy (antibiotics or antiviral drugs) often leads to no or just mild deficits in learning and memory.

Practical Example

A businessperson shows acute confusion and is admitted to a regional hospital. The first medication with an antivirustatic drug shows no effect and is replaced. Rehabilitation takes place in a closed/protected ward because of the severe amnestic syndrome and acute tendency to wander off. After several months, the woman is discharged home, into the care of her husband. The husband takes a leave of absence from work. The neuroleptic medication is discontinued. The patient shows no explicit learning and memory performance (but an intact memory span), but is able to do more and more things in her daily life with less and less guidance (e.g. personal hygiene, making breakfast). The husband is specifically guided neuropsychologically with regard to compensation and shaping of the living environment. ◄

6.8   Hydrocephalus and Normal Pressure Hydrocephalus (NPH)

The brain and the spinal cord are surrounded by cerebrospinal fluid (CSF) in- and outside. This stabilizes and protects the brain from shock. It neutralizes the force of gravity. The brain is figuratively swimming in this fluid. Every day, several hundred millilitres of new fluid are produced in special cells and must be drained off. Otherwise there is a risk of damaging pressure on the brain and spinal cord.

A change in CSF **circulation** (e.g. acquired constriction, anatomical variation) results in pressure or negative pressure that damages brain function. Prolonged alteration of CSF outflow cause severe cognitive deficits (e.g. dementia) with emphasis on learning and memory. After a timely lumbar puncture or shunt installation (artificial drainage), the performance of those affected often improves significantly. Acute improvements (e.g. reaction time, walking performance, memory performance) are sometimes seen about 24 h after a lumbar puncture.

The therapy is oriented towards the chronicity and severity of the learning and memory disorders. In the early phase of therapy, the focus is on exercises and the teaching of strategies. In the late phases of therapy, cognitive stimulating methods can be applied. However, the focus is on counselling and compensatory techniques (e.g. notes, smartphone).

Significant learning and memory deficits in children, adolescents and adults are usually the result of acquired brain damage.

Dementia 7

Dementia is a severe syndrome resulting from a chronic or progressive degeneration of the brain (e.g. Darby & Walsh, 2005). It is caused by progressive degeneration (usually **atrophy**) in subcortical or cortical areas. A diagnosis of dementia includes an assessment of the duration of problems (over 6 months). Affected individuals and their families need counseling. Contact points are the treating physicians, neuropsychologists, specialized centers at neurological clinics and self-help groups.

7.1 Alzheimer's Disease

This most common form of dementia is characterized by cell death in the area of the temporal lobe and the hippocampus. Neuropathologically, **amyloid deposits** (β-amyloid is deposited in and on nerve cells; amyloid plaques) and **neurofibrils** can be detected, which cause nerve cells death. The slowly progressive course leads to severe cognitive impairment with a frequent primary focus on learning and memory impairment. This leads to massive impairment of everyday activities. Particularly relevant and burdensome are the personality and behavioural changes present in later stages and the accompanying cognitive-affective complaints such as depression, insomnia, incontinence, illusions, hallucinations, delusions, sudden aggressive outbursts and sexual dysfunctions.

Dementia screening procedures (see below) hardly detect slight impairments and do not replace a detailed neuropsychological examination. Regarding cognition an increased rate of forgetting over time, i.e. delayed recall, is already evident at an early stage. Furthermore, there are errors in recognition, deficits in working memory and in cognitive flexibility. Occupational therapy, physical therapy, speech therapy and neuropsychological therapy can be helpful (especially in the early phase). Only in the disease's early and middle phase drug therapies (so-called Antidementiva) seem to have a helpful effect. In general, multidimensional approaches are recommended. They have the best evidence.

Practical Example

A geriatric nurse shows increasing forgetfulness and is admitted to a regional hospital. There, an incipient Alzheimer's disease is diagnosed. The patient shows decreasing explicit learning and memory performance (with intact memory span), and can perform less and less things in the course of time (e.g. personal hygiene, making breakfast). The husband is specifically guided with regard to compensation and shaping of the living environment (e.g. pleasant activities, relaxation, biography work, reminiscence work). ◄

7.2   Ischaemic Vascular Dementia (IVD)

This form (formerly called multi-infarct dementia) is characterized by progressive learning and memory disorders due to vascular disorders (macrovascular as well as microvascular). **Gradual** deterioration is typical. Symptoms are highly variable depending on the position of the lesion (see blood supply). Alternatively, subcortical structures are affected by circulatory disturbances. Moreover, there are also mixed forms of Alzheimer's and vascular dementia.

Dementia screening procedures (see below) hardly detect mild impairments and do not replace a detailed neuropsychological examination. Affected people and their families should definitely seek advice. Occupational therapy, physiotherapy, speech therapy and neuropsychological therapy can be helpful, especially in the early phase.

7.3   Dementia in Parkinson's Disease (PDD)

Due to a change in neurotransmitter concentration (dopamine deficiency) in the basal ganglia (especially substantia nigra), but also in the olfactory cells and nerve cells in the intestine, there are impairments in motor coordination (e.g. resting tremor, rigor, akinesia) and slowed information processing. In one-third of Parkinson patients, a development of dementia is seen. Executive dysfunction (reduced cognitive flexibility) often occurs in an early phase of the disease. Moreover, there is often increased tiredness, so called "fatigue". In further phases, there are often restlessness and considerable affective changes (often with depressive episodes and anxiety). Also distressing are hallucinations (visual, usually complex, fleshed-out perceptions of people, animals, or objects) and paranoid delusions (often-regarding infidelity). The primary disease and side effects of the medication interact. Very rarely, a corresponding syndrome develops after brain injury or due to medication.

Neuropsychological assessment reveals disturbances in learning and memory (caudate nucleus), in executive functions (e.g. planning, initiating actions, flexibility, word fluency) and in attention (information processing speed, so-called "Bradyphrenia").

7.4 Dementia in Huntington's Disease

This very rare and hereditary form of dementia (autosomal dominant; genetic defect on chromosome 4, males and females suffer equally) leads to severe learning and memory disorders often in the fourth decade of life. Often severe personality changes and motor disorders (so-called St. Vitus dance) are characteristic. Patients usually die within 15 years of diagnosis. Symptoms can be temporarily alleviated by therapy (occupational, physical and speech therapy) and medication (e.g. neuroleptics, antiparkinsonian drugs, antidepressants).

7.5 Dementia in Creutzfeld-Jakob Disease

Creutzfeldt-Jakob disease is extremely rare and represents a "sporadic" form (i.e. without a clear cause). In addition, there is a hereditary form and a form acquired through infection. Because of the possible infectious nature, tissues and body fluids of affected individuals are considered potentially infectious. There is no known effective treatment and most sufferers die within a year. Affected individuals benefit from occupational therapy, speech therapy, and physical therapy. Behavioral problems are treated symptomatically with psychotropic drugs.

7.6   Other Neurological Diseases

7.6.1   Multiple Sclerosis (MS)

Today, this term is used to describe a wide range of different forms of the disease. Depending on the onset and course of the disease, subtypes are distinguished. The physical and cognitive symptoms are based on inflammation of the myelin sheaths of the nerve cells.

Depending on the localization of the lesion, corresponding deficits then become apparent. Learning and memory disorders are extremely variable and fluctuate over time. General cognitive deficits are seen in about 50–60% of the patients. Accordingly, a differentiated neuropsychological diagnosis is indicated. Multidisciplinary therapeutic approaches including neuropsychological therapy are advisable.

In the cognitive field, the often present **"fatigue"** influences learning and memory performance. Psychotherapy, compensatory approaches and psychoeducation (planned break management "Pacing") are often the main part of therapy.

7.7   Wernicke-Korsakow-Syndrome and Wernicke's Encephalopathy

This disorder is characterized by severe anterograde and retrograde amnesia (Darby & Walsh, 2005). Temporally, the **encephalopathy** precedes the **Korsakow syndrome.** Only very early treatment of the encephalopathy (including abstinence from alcohol!) can prevent a syndrome. Anatomically, there are small hemorrhages in the vascular walls of the brain and a massive damage in the diencephalon (especially the mammillary bodies). The cause is usually chronic and intensive alcohol consumption with associated thiamine deficiency (Vitamin B1) and other malnutrition.

Clinically severe behavioural disturbances and a tendency to **confabulation** become apparent. Memory gaps are filled with often nonsensical and seemingly freely associated content. Depending on the severity of the memory disorder and associated personality changes (e.g. impulse control disorder, disinhibition), attempts of correction do not help. Distraction is often an effective strategy of de-escalation. Medicinal treatment is often useful in parallel.

Counselling of relatives plays an important role in the overall concept. Closed inpatient care is often helpful and necessary.

In the clinical context, a combination of Wernicke-Korsakow-Syndrome and a TBI under alcohol is more frequent. In these patients, the motivation for therapy or the self-awareness is often massively disturbed. The prognosis is unfavourable.

Practical Example

A middle-aged man drinks large amounts of alcohol over a period of years, loses his job and his wife and separates from her. Neglect ensues, which the ex-wife notices and therefore initiates legal care. Mr. X. requires long-term inpatient psychiatric care and is only able to manage his daily life with massive nursing support. Mr. X. shows retrograde amnesia for years and severe antero-grade amnesia with impaired memory span and massive deficits in all other learning and memory areas. In addition, there are confabulation and severe impulse control disorders, some of which require neuroleptic treatment. ◄

Checklist 2: Other Causes of Learning and Memory Disorders

- Hypothyroidism and hypoparathyroidism
- Vitamin deficiency diseases B1, B6, B12 and folic acid
- Metabolic encephalopathies (exclusion by clinical diagnostics)
- Chronic liver diseases (Wilson's disease, hemochromatosis, cirrhosis)
- Chronic kidney disease (dialysis encephalopathy)
- Intoxications (exclusion by clinical and laboratory diagnostics)
- Industrial toxins (e.g. carbon monoxide, mercury, lead, perchloroethy-lene)
- Electrolyte disorders (exclusion by clinical and laboratory diagnostics)
- Hematological disorders (exclusion by clinical and laboratory diagnostics)
- Polycythaemia, hyperlipidaemia, multiple myeloma, anaemia
- Late forms of leukodystrophies, e.g. ceroid lipofuscinosis (exclusion by clinical and laboratory diagnostics)
- Cannabis use (THC)

Various forms of dementia and other neurological diseases often cause severe and progressive disturbances of learning and memory.

Reference

Darby, D., & Walsh, K. (2005). *Neuropsychology. A clinical approach* (5th ed.). Elsevier.

Diagnostics and Assessment

8

Multidisciplinary therapy begins with assessment and other diagnostic procedures.

> **Checklist 3: Memory Deficits (See Also Checklists 1 and 2)**
>
> - Anamnesis (Do biographical indications of brain damage exist?), external anamnesis and initial symptoms
> - Medication/drugs and physical examination (e.g. dehydration)
> - Psychological examination (e.g. depression/individual factors) and neuropsychological diagnosis with behavioural observation and external and self-assessment scales (see ICF; Fig. 1.1)
> - Environmental factors (Favourable? Unfavourable?; see Fig. 1.1)
> - Laboratory and cerebrospinal fluid diagnostics and, if necessary, cerebral imaging (CT, MRT), EEG and sonography of the vessels supplying the brain

8.1 Communication with Affected Persons

During greeting and explanation of the procedure, the **reason for** the examination is explained ("Your wife is worried about you"). The language is adapted individually. If there is a language barrier, native-speaking examiners are optimal. The use of a translator involves clear disadvantages (possibly distortion of the instruction or unauthorized assistance).

© The Author(s), under exclusive license to Springer Fachmedien
Wiesbaden GmbH, part of Springer Nature 2023
V. Völzke, *Patients with Memory Disorders*, essentials,
https://doi.org/10.1007/978-3-658-39800-2_8

Asking about **complaints** and their development (anamnesis) is done freely or by means of structured interviews with closed or open questions. Often patients report short-term memory disorders. They are unable to remember current episodes, i.e. episodes that occurred a short time ago, and especially things that need to be done (prospective memory).

Tests are announced and administered without pressure. Many affected persons ask whether it is a "test for idiots". We use an explanation about the usefulness of the procedures. They are a starting point for a possible therapy. Often a comparison with a medical blood test or X-ray is helpful ("The tests allow a comparison with other people their age. The aim is to explore, which performances are currently intact and which areas, if any, are impaired.").

During the examination, the **test instructions** and **standards** must be focused. It can be useful to give feedback only **cautiously** and to focus the **therapeutic alliance**. This is important especially in severely affected persons, affected persons with a disorder of illness insight (Prigatano, 1999) or paranoid affected persons. The therapeutic alliance is highly relevant, particularly for sufferers with dementia or sufferers in the acute or post-acute phase of the illness or rehabilitation. Deficits should not be minimized at the same time. Communication should be individually adapted, appreciative, sufficiently slow and adaptively detailed. It is important that no feelings of guilt be connoted to the patient.

8.2   Assessment Instruments

The selection in Table 8.1 does not include purely **computer-based** procedures. These are usually part of a test system and require special hardware and software components. Furthermore, the focus was placed on frequently used and relatively newly standardized or very established procedures in clinical practice. Procedures that are more **experimental, assessment scales, old memory tests** and autobiographical test procedures were **not** considered.

There are special tasks for children and young people. The VLMT and the Complex-Figure-Test have already been described. Learning and memory tests are often integrated into general test batteries (see Table 8.2).

Screening tests are popular and easily available. They may only be used for the appropriately normed age group. They do **not** replace **a** detailed neuropsychological examination (Table 8.3).

Table 8.1 Memory tests for adults (selection)

Name	Standardization and duration	Description	Note
Rivermead Behavioural Memory Test (RBMT-III) by Wilson et al. (2008)	Normalization from 16 to 90 years; no educational norms; duration up to 30 min	9 subtests (including text reproduction) with different tasks in a fixed order with high relevance to everyday life	Test for the assessment of episodic and prospective memory functions (differentiated assessment of severe disorders)
California Verbal Learning and Retention Test (CVLT-III) by Delis et al. (2017)	Normalization from 20 to 60 years; data for three school-leaving qualifications and men and women; duration with delay 60 min; two parallel forms	Learning a word list with 16 items, distraction list and delayed retrieval with and without cue stimuli and recognition	Suitable for recording even slight deficits; supplementary recording of benefits through categorization (kitchen utensils, fish etc.)
Wechsler Memory Test (WMS-R IV) by Wechsler (2009)	Normalization from 16 to 90 years; duration with delay 75 min	13 subtests (recording different types of memory and retrieval modalities)	Suitable for recording moderate deficits
CERAD (consortium to establish a registry for Alzheimer's disease) Engl. by neuropsychological test battery (CERAD-NP) of geriatric medicine at the university of Basel	Normalization sample average 69 years	Various subtests: Mini mental status examination, word list (learning, recall, recognition); figures (signing, recall) and plus tests	Test battery for the assessment of cognitive deficits in old age (including dementia processes). Freely available for qualified personnel
Complex Figure Test (CFT) by Meyers and Meyers (1996) or parallel forms as memory task	International norms see Lezak et al. (2012) or Strauss et al. (2006).	Learning phase (copying task) and then free recall immediately (3 min) or after a time delay (depending on standardization)	Procedure for the detection of non-verbal learning disorders; cautious interpretation in case of parallel spatial-constructive disorders

(continued)

Table 8.1 (continued)

Name	Standardization and duration	Description	Note
Wechsler Adult Intelligence Test (WAIS-IV) by Wechsler (2010) with the memory subtests.	Normalization from 16 to 89; 11 years. Evaluation of total scores in value points or evaluation of maximum reproduced items (see below). Data from the norming sample in the manual and many international norms	Forward number recall (memory span), backward number recall (working memory), and sequential number recall (working memory).	Frequently used procedure (part in several test batteries)
			Captures working memory; people with educational disabilities show memory-independent deficits
		Letter-number sequences (working memory): Mentally sorting letters and numbers	
Block tapping test (Corsi????)	Normalization of the span of memory from 15 years	Measurement of visual spatial memory span and working memory	Affected persons with visual disturbances or visual field defects show correspondingly associated insecurities

Table 8.2 Memory tests for children and adolescents (selection)

Name	Standardization and duration	Description	Note
Wechsler Intelligence Scale for Children – Fifth Edition (WISC-V) by Wechsler (2014)	Subtests from 3 to 14 years	Repeating numbers and letter-number sequences (see above)	

Table 8.3 Screening procedures and tests for special groups

Name	Standardization and duration	Description	Note
Mini-Mental-State Examination (MMSE; original Folstein et al. 1975)	Standards without reference to age	Learning 3 words; delayed free query	Freely available on the internet or from pharmaceutical companies.
			Suitable as an initial short test. Integrated into other tasks
Montreal cognitive assessment (MOCA)	Standards, among others, at www. memoryclinic.ch	Word list of 5 items read out twice and recalled after a time delay of 5 min; number repeat forward (5 items) and backward (3 items)	Freely available on the internet or from pharmaceutical companies.
			Suitable as an initial short test. Integrated into other tasks
Parkinson Neuropsychometric Dementia Assessment (PANDA) by Kalbe et al. (2008)	Normalization up to 59 and from 60 years	Reading aloud of 5 word pairs and immediate recall three times; time-delayed recall; backward number repeat up to 6 items	Freely available on the internet or from pharmaceutical companies.
			Suitable as initial short test

References (Overview)

Delis, D. C., Kramer, J. H., Kaplan, E., & Ober, B. A. (2017). *Manual for the California verbal learning test, 3rd edition (CVLT-III)*. The Psychological Corporation.

Folstein, M. F., Folstein, S. E., & McHugh, P. R. (1975). "Mini-Mental-State". A practical method for grading the cognitive state for clinician. *Journal of Psychiatric Research, 12*, 189–198.

Kalbe, E., Calabrese, P., Kohn, N., Hilker, R., Riedel, O., Wittchen, H., Dodel, R., Otto, J., Ebersbach, G., & Kessler, J. (2008). Screening for cognitive deficits in Parkinson's disease with the Parkinson neuropsychometric dementia assessment (PANDA) Instrument. *Parkinsonism & Related Disorders, 14*, S.93–S101. https://doi.org/10.1016/j.parkreldis.2007.06.008

Lezak, M., Howieson, D., Bigler, E., & Tranel, D. (2012). *Neuropsychological Assessment* (5. Aufl.). Oxford University Press.

Meyers, J., & Meyers, K. (1996). *Rey complex figure and the recognition trial. Professional manual. Supplemental norms for children and adolescents.* Psychological Assessment Resources.

Prigatano, G. (1999). *Principles of neuropsychological rehabilitation.* University Press.

Strauss, E., Sherman, E., & Spreen, O. (2006). *A compendium of neuropsychological tests* (3. Aufl.). Oxford University Press.

Wechsler, D. (2009). *The Wechsler Memory Scale-4th edition (WMS-IV).* Pearson Assessments.

Wechsler, D. (2010). *The Wechsler Adult Intelligence Scale – 4th edition (WAIS-IV).* Pearson Assessments.

Wechsler, D. (2014). *The Wechsler Adult Intelligence Scale for Children – 5th Edition (WISC-V).* San Antonio, TX: Pearson Assessments.

Wilson, B., Greenfield, E., Clare, L., Baddeley, A., Cockburn, J., Watson, P., Tate, R., Sopena, S., & Nannery, R. (2008). *Rivermead behavioural memory test* (3rd ed.). Pearson Assessment.

Basics of Exercises and Therapy

Memory therapy (e.g. Winson et al., 2017), exercises, and training or "brain jogging" are available in multiple variants. Often, more or less simple **memory tasks** with a memorization and recall phases are performed. These can be purchased in magazines, books and as a program or app or can also be used free of charge. However, memory is not a muscle that only needs to be trained (Winson et al., 2017). In neuropsychological (psycho)therapy in individual therapy, in groups with or without computer programs or apps, on the other hand specific memory aspects are treated **(strategy development).**

Therapy is based on **neuroplasticity,** the transmission of **information** and **adaptation/design of** the learning as well on the living environment. In literature (e.g. Winson et al., 2017; Prigatano, 1999) the terms **cognitive stimulation** and therapy are used. They differ in terms of specificity and have fluid transitions. The effectiveness of cognitive stimulation has been studied in particular in healthy elderly people (resilience, prevention of dementia, etc.). Significant effects are generally seen here. There is only limited transfer to non-trained areas.

There are therapeutic procedures that serve as a form of **functional restoration** (recovery of the systems, etc.). The effective factor is **repetition** (i.e. repetition of exercises) with sufficient intensity. The aim is the partial or complete reactivation of networks (plasticity) which are not too severely impaired. In parallel, there is the adaptation of exercises in terms of difficulty to the performance limit (shaping). A distinction is also made between non-specific approaches for stimulation (listening to the radio, etc.), targeted "bottom-up" approaches (i.e. exercises), concept-oriented "top-down" approaches (including attention therapy with strategy and the communication of background knowledge, taking into account the self-assessment of affected patients), stimulation of inhibitory processes (in which a second

V. Völzke, *Patients with Memory Disorders*, essentials, https://doi.org/10.1007/978-3-658-39800-2_9

neuronal system is activated) and stimulation of attentional components (if necessary, improvement of activation, i. e. medication).

The shorter the period since the onset of the illness or the event, the more effective are exercise procedures. In parallel, the therapeutic work includes aspects of **self-assessment** and **self-efficiency** (What helps me?). After a longer period of therapy or after the event, compensatory procedures are primarily indicated. Since 2012, in Germany outpatient **neuropsychological therapy** has become a health insurance benefit and may start up to 5 years after an event. A later start of therapy requires a separate application with detailed justification.

Compensation includes tools (i.e. **external**, including assistance systems), new strategies (i.e. **internal**), but also increased effort. A strategy must be transparent, sensible and clear. Severely affected patients often cannot use strategies because of the complexity. They can only use help if there is a basal insight and resilience. On the other hand, mildly affected patients often lack insight into the necessity of therapy, especially in an early phase of the disease.

Furthermore, there are **integrated procedures** that explicitly combine classic psychotherapeutic procedures (e.g. self-instruction, role-playing) with exercise procedures. For the therapy of learning and memory disorders, as for all other approaches, the SMART rule applies as far as possible. SMART is an acronym for **specific**, **measurable**, **accepted**, **relevant** and **scheduled**.

> Exercises and therapy are based on different processes and are often combined in practice.

9.1   Therapy Setting

Therapy begins in the **acute phase** or **early rehabilitation.** Patients with a tendency to "wander" and severe cognitive deficits require a protective setting. During the acute stay, fixation and drug therapy are the only options.

As part of early and continuing rehabilitation, a number of special wards for amnesic patients are available in Germany (e.g. Hattingen and Pulsnitz). They offer the appropriate protection and specialized multidisciplinary therapy to the affected persons. In a separate follow-up study in Hattingen, 16 patients show improvements in participation, awareness, cooperation, communication and attention within 4 weeks, but not in explicit memory (Hein, 2017). Depending on age, resilience, family and financial situation, home reintegration, a residential group for people with acquired brain injury (e.g. Bielefeld Bethel, Germany), a residential group for people with dementia, long-term rehabilitation (e.g. Berlin) or a closed or open nursing home are integrated into the planning for this group. Relatives need long-term support (advice and concrete help). Professional helpers need further training (e.g. neuropsychology, de-escalation) and often supervision. In different states, very different systems of rehabilitation exist.

9.2 Therapy of Learning and Memory Disorders

An overview is provided by Hildebrandt (2019) or Winson et al. (2017). The **atmosphere is shaped by** understanding, accepting, and a freedom of anxiety. In this regard a medium level of arousal represents the optimal base for therapy. Consider principles of **reinforcement** (reward), **motivational research** (e.g. motives, attribution), and the effect of primacy and recency (impressions). Start the therapy session with a friendly and personal greeting and, if possible, end the therapy session with success and praise.

Treatment planning includes the evaluation of the individual test results (see Checklist 4) and all other areas (e.g. age, prognosis, environmental factors, personal resources). It is very important to distinguish between severe, moderate and mild memory disorders.

Checklist 4: Parallel Existing Disturbances

- Attention deficits (e.g. fatigue, distractibility)
- Executive disorders (e.g. inefficient strategy)
- Spatial disturbances (e.g. spatial neglect)
- Personality changes (e.g. lack of effort, awareness of deficit)
- Speech disorders (e.g. reading disability)

Simplifying, exercise procedures are effective for mild memory disorders. They improve attention and resilience. This approach is based on appropriate motivation and meta-cognitive knowledge (e.g. introspection, awareness).

You can use **anatomical models** (if necessary, paint them yourself) and simplified information (**guidebooks**). They support feedback of test results and the therapy planning (see guidebook). They can be integrated into an information folder (**external help/internal strategies).**

At the same time, considerations are made (if necessary also with relatives) about **priorities** in everyday life. Therefore the "ICF model" and the "SMART rule" are useful. Steps are the **analysis** of the (problem) situation, **exploration** of the motivation, the **development** of strategy (**information sheet**) and the **practice** of this strategy.

In **severe** and possibly moderate disorders, different **compensatory** approaches are useful. It depends on the duration of the deficits and prognosis. In parallel cognitive stimulation therapy (e.g. games, attention tasks) is often useful.

9.3   Practical Approaches for Memory Therapy

9.3.1   Exercises

Therapy programs and **apps** include verbal and figural tasks.
Examples of memory tasks in programs/apps (selection):

- Number Repetition
- Arithmetic approaches (e.g. $3 + 4 + 5 + 6 =$??)
- Remembering and reordering sequences of pictures
- Remembering positions of figures
- Identifying "new-or-not-new" images
- Learning of shopping lists

Many analogue paper-pencil tasks are available. There is an unmanageable variety of task collections. They are available in bookshops and sometimes even in supermarkets. The term "memory training" usually refers to a collection of cognitive exercises, often including perceptual, attentional and executive exercises.

It is evident that pure memorization and practice without strategy leads to frustration (Winson et al., 2017).

> **Practical Example**
>
> A patient after a craniocerebral trauma trained a spatial memory task (flashing dice) excessively without therapeutic guidance and improved a lot. In everyday life, however, there was no improvement in participation and tests (e.g. recall of the CFT). ◄

Working memory exercises complete the repertoire. The "N-back paradigm" is often used. If the actual stimulus (e.g. numbers, letters, animals) is the same as the stimulus N-positions before the trainee needs to press a key. The degree of difficulty is adaptable. The transfer to other cognitive domains (e.g. "distant transfer" to learning to read, intelligence) or long-term effects is unclear for different age groups (Melby-Lervåg et al., 2016). The exercises are used as cognitive stimulation.

Analogous to the **N-Back method,** paper-pencil tasks or games are available. The critical stimulus (e.g. black card colour) that appeared N-before positions needs to be detected. Paper-pencil tasks include arithmetic tasks in which the intermediate result must be stored in the mind in order to solve a second task.

Example:

5 × 8 =

6 × 9 =

Subtract the Lower Value from the Upper Value Without Writing Down the Intermediate Results

The complexity of the exercises can be easily changed. In **card games,** working memory can be trained by laying cards and tapping whenever the current colour or symbol is identical to the penultimate card. Simple increases in complexity are possible.

Another exercise in working memory is **counting or spelling backwards** in varying steps (e.g. from 111 backwards in steps of 4) or longer words. The complexity is increased by performing another operation with the respective letter (e.g. saying the first letter of a city). **Parallel tasks** also train the working memory (e.g. memorizing a text and parallel underlining of defined letters). Subjective improvements or test improvements are probably based on **improved attention processes** and **improved insight into the disease.**

Learning requires **repetition.** Reading aloud or repetition itself is not very effective. It is important to link the information and store multimodal (Winson et al., 2017). The **mnemonics technique** that has been used for centuries is a form of visualization using the loci method. Here, elements to be remembered are placed there during a mental walk through a very well known place and then recalled accordingly. This technique is suitable for healthy people and people with mild disorders without other cognitive deficits. If necessary, an adapted **self-instruction training** (from external to internal) is suitable for practicing all techniques.

Often we do exercises with **texts.** The aim is to improve the **depth of processing** by reflecting prior knowledge, asking questions, active reading, text repetition and its review. Applicable is also a kind of "W-Question-Technique" (Who is mentioned? Where did it happen? What happened? What are the consequences?).

A technique which is easy to learn is the **loud telling of** learning content to another person. Here, the information is structured internally **(processing depth)** and additionally heard **(multimodal).** During the telling it becomes clear what is still uncertainly represented. The visualization of the learning content can be supported by **pictorial imagining or** painting. Well-structured learning groups with two or more people are very effective. Alternatively, learning content can be dictated onto a smartphone and controlled. This technique is suitable for healthy people and those affected with **mild** disorders and without accompanying deficits.

An adolescent following SHT and mild memory impairment (VLMT) benefits from this approach by improving depth of processing, supplementation with visualization, and frequent feedback from the study group. ◄

In the psychotherapeutic context or in the implementation of homework, the client is asked to **repeat** or **verbalize** what they understood or remembered (**written homework and summaries if necessary**). In the case of memory disorders, it is even more important to make the procedure transparent.

The **place of learning** is important for people with cognitive disorders. Distraction and interference influence learning success. If the place of learning is linked to negative emotions, these will be recurrent (classical conditioning). Learning success also depends on the strength of arousal. The optimal learning success is achieved with medium arousal. Too much calm or fear have a negative effect.

Learning and therapy groups (Wilson et al., 2017) motivate (especially children and adolescents) and include feedback (improving self-assessment).

Material for and content of memory therapy (Winson et al., 2017) including working materials:

- How memory works (anatomy, priorities and strategy)
- Remembering names (e.g. associations, rhymes, origin of the name)
- Structuring of information (generic terms of products to buy)
- Retention of auditory information (pre-structuring according to areas)
- Reading and retaining texts (prior knowledge, asking questions, active reading, repeating text, checking)
- External memory aids (collection of possibilities)
- Pictorial imagination (e.g. tree)
- Story techniques (with pictorial imagination)
- Remembering numbers (e.g. grouping, typing patterns, rhymes)

The planned management of **breaks** and **learning phases** is important. Individuals (including psychotherapy clients) often have lack knowledge in this area. Knowledge (meta-cognitive) about one's own strengths and weaknesses and the ability to assess the complexity of tasks are important.

Very **short breaks** are useful during learning (e.g. stretching, standing). After approximately 20–30 min, there should be a first short break (maximum 5 min). After a maximum of 2 h, a **longer** break of approximately 20 min is useful. Movements lead to recovery. After 4 h at the latest, an even longer break is advisable (1–2 h). Often this recommendation contradicts the previous learning routine.

Motivation for learning and therapy is crucial. Sufficient motivation and re-inforcement create a medium level of arousal and a good foundation. People attri-bute their success or failure to different causes. An analysis of the functionality of the styles (what is helpful?) is important for the therapy (controllability, temporal stability and internality or externality). Persons with a failure avoidance need spe-cial counselling. Clients can learn to control relevant factors and individual knowl-edge can be acquired. The own effort can be modified and supporting resources (e.g. equipment, people) are identified.

The **errorless learning concept** implies avoidance of false memories and the use of cueing stimuli. It is used in the therapy of patients with memory disorders.

Repetitions can be staggered (spaced retrieval) by first repeating the informa-tion after 1, then after 2, 5 and 10 min.

9.3.2 Compensation and External Aid

It can be useful to **delegate tasks** to other people (e.g. "Remind me often, please!") and to **ask for repetition** (e.g. "Could you please repeat this again."). It is helpful to **involve caregivers** (e.g., "I know I can't remember everything. That is why I focus on certain content. Please help me!").

Notes and slips of paper belong to the everyday compensation techniques and help if they are used in a structured way (e.g. identical storage location). They are suitable for people with mild deficits.

Notebooks, memory diaries and **calendars** help if the notes are integrated into a routine (control of the notes and implementation of the activities to be done). Especially people who have always used diaries benefit from this method.

Electronic calendars (possibly with a large keyboard) offer advantages over paper calendars. They are modern "notepads" and contain reminder functions (spe-cial appointments and routines). Patients with mild or moderate deficits can also add appointments themselves. Patients with severe deficits need sufficient support in entering, recalling and, above all, implementing the appointments. Ideally, ther-apists and relatives are well acquainted with the respective program.

Stimulus control involves learning in a quiet, low-stimulus environment. People often need counselling to change their learning routines (e.g. no reading and listening to the radio at the same time). **Inhibition/disturbance** of learning content (interference) should be prevented. Learning requires time for storage and consolidation (e.g. attention deficits especially deficits in sustained attention).

Routines reduce the cognitive capacity required to complete tasks. Trained rou-tines help even patients with a severe amnestic syndrome after weeks and months. They enable them to cope with everyday life.

Visual representations are particularly effective. Visualizations can help to better store contents of therapy and counselling (e.g. board pictures, symbolizations, creative drawings). A painted snail can symbolize a thoughtful and decelerated way of working. A shamrock can be a symbol of confident cognition. For complex content, diagrams can help to simplify complex relationships. In case of severe memory deficits a **daily photo calendar** (smartphone) can help to reconstruct the individual day (with the relatives) and gives security.

The support of **relatives** and their **counselling** are very important and necessary.

> **Role of Relatives**
>
> • Providing structure, emotional relief and understanding
> • Guide and support internal and external strategies
> • Explain the reasonableness of the measures

9.3.3 Therapy of Severe Memory Disorders (Including Dementia)

Despite the imposing memory disorders, we continue to place the **individual person** at the centre of our therapeutic efforts.

The care and therapy of people with severe memory disorders (including dementia) is primarily concerned with maintaining basic functions in everyday life (e.g. eating, dressing, communicating). Components are a pharmacological therapy, especially an appropriate design of the environment, continence training and a sufficient or adapted diet. Often, after neurological or psychiatric diagnosis, anti-dementia or behavior-modulating drugs (including neuroleptics) are justified. Especially for **caring relatives, the care team** or therapists, even a slight improvement in the problem areas can be extremely relevant and significant. The therapy options are generally very limited and the therapy programs focus on the preservation of cognitive and other abilities (e.g. biography work with validation, self-preservation).

Design of a Therapy Unit

In therapy, we work with people with severe perceptual disorders. Both the perception of the outside world and the inner world can be affected in the context of dementia or severe memory disorders. The aim is to compensate the various deficits. Caregivers and relatives shape the relationship. Routines help in everyday life and provide structure.

Helpful Basic Settings

We base our work on basic needs (according to Kitwood, 1992, 2008). We provide comfort with warmth, tenderness, security and a sense of safety. Regardless of age we need primary attachment. The need for primary security and employment remain. Without employment, skills begin to decline ("use it or lose it"). People, especially thofse with severe memory disorders, have a need for identity or life story. We provide this by biography work (e.g. life stories). People with severe memory deficits perceive friendliness, politeness and emotional tones despite all deficits and often retain this aspect in memory as well (implicit learning).

Checklist 5: Dealing with People with Severe Amnestic Syndrome or Dementia

- Always reintroduce yourself and build trust by starting the conversation with an appreciative message.
- Create awareness and links to previous experiences.
- Avoid "baby talk". Speak clearly in simple concrete sentences and get to the point as soon as possible.
- Ask easy questions that can be answered with yes or no.
- Do not unsettle them by frequently asking for facts that are not recallable. It shames.
- Body signals can give indications of the emotional state. If necessary, address the emotional level of patients with dementia ("They feel completely alone").
- Pain, stress and anxiety trigger impulsive actions or aggression.
- The view of the person with dementia is in a subjective perspective valid and correct.
- Do not interpret the aggression of the person with dementia to yourself, even if he directs the aggression towards you.
- Lectures, rebukes and fruitless discussions do not help.
- Touching or holding may be inappropriate in response to aggression and irritability. Remain calm. Keep distance if necessary. Show up with your side view rather than front body view. Get help.
- Distract instead of confront. Maintain patience and composure.
- Give instructions in single steps one after the other and repeat instructions.

Advice for Relatives

People with severe memory disorders need compensation (see above), the provision of security and the appropriate shaping of their life situation.

> **Overview**
> **Exercise:** Please visualize the needs of the person concerned.
> An explicit memory of the contents of conversations is missing. The security in everyday life is lost. Routines become uncertain, to say the least. Even the performance of everyday tasks becomes difficult. At the same time, I wish security, attention, closeness. Every confrontation with everyday matters and possibly existential issues makes me feel even more insecure and at the same time, I lack the cognitive resources to deal with them.

Joint appointments with the patient and partner are an option. The prerequisite is, of course, an explicit agreement with the patient/client and, if necessary, a written agreement. Homework or other agreements can additionally be fixed in writing.

Practical Example

An elderly woman with declining memory after hydrocephalus repeatedly complains that she is often very unfair to her husband. The husband corrects the frequency of the episodes and assures his affection and understanding. ◄

In most families or relationships, there are **unsolved issues** and **legacies** (e.g. disappointments, violence) that often involve slights. People with memory disorders are usually not able to discuss these "difficult issues". It makes no sense to assert one's own needs. The impaired person cannot actively participate and rather needs protection.

Don't Test the Affected Person

Relatives always want to know whether the impaired person can (re)recall episodes or facts. In this case, the person is repeatedly put under pressure and forced to answer without having the necessary knowledge. The consequences may be "confabulation" and emotional stress. This leads to restlessness or aggressiveness.

It is much better to provide the patient with sufficient information:

- I repeatedly mention the current day
- I report the experiences
- I use old knowledge (biography work) and the remaining resources

References (Overview)

Hein, C. (2017). *Patientenstudie zu Veränderungen kognitiver und affektiver Parameter bei Patienten mit schwerem amnestischen Syndrom unterschiedlicher Ätiologie in der Rehabilitation Eine empirische Studie mit einer besonderen Patientengruppe.* Masterarbeit an der Fernuniversität Hagen.

Hildebrandt, H. (2019). *Cognitive rehabilitation of memory.* Academic Press.

Kitwood, T., & Bredin, K. (1992). Towards a theory of dementia care: Personhood and well-being. *Ageing and Society, 12*(3), 269–287. https://doi.org/10.1017/S0144686X0000502X

Kitwood, T. (2008). *Demenz. Der person-zentrierte Ansatz im Umgang mit verwirrten Menschen.* Huber.

Melby-Lervåg, M., Redick, T. S., & Hulme, C. (2016). Working memory training does not improve performance on measures of intelligence or other measures of "far transfer": evidence from a meta-analytic review. *Perspectives on Psychological Science: A Journal of the Association for Psychological Science, 11*(4), 512–534. https://doi.org/10.1177/1745691616635612

Prigatano, G. (1999). *Principles of neuropsychological rehabilitation.* University Press.

Winson, R., Wilson, B., & Bateman, A. (2017). *The brain injury rehabilitation workbook.* Guilford Press.

Summary

10

Learning and memory disorders influence the psychotherapeutic process in a special way. Figure 10.1 summarizes conclusions.

© The Author(s), under exclusive license to Springer Fachmedien
Wiesbaden GmbH, part of Springer Nature 2023
V. Völzke, *Patients with Memory Disorders*, essentials,
https://doi.org/10.1007/978-3-658-39800-2_10

Fig. 10.1 Summary of the
impact of learning and
memory disorders on the
psychotherapeutic process

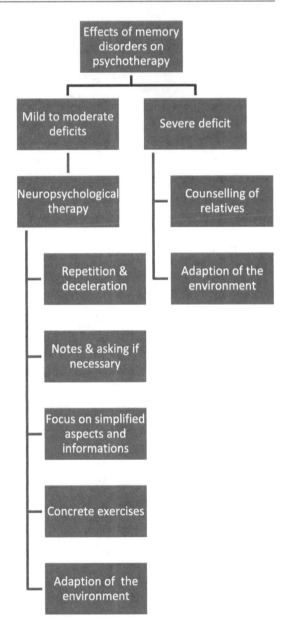

What You Can Take Away from This *Essential*

- Clear criteria which diagnostic and therapeutic options exist
- Well-founded overview of which temporary and chronic causes of memory disorders there may be
- Understandable explanation of what compensatory measures can look like in the case of severe memory impairment
- Helpful suggestions on what to look for when counselling family members
- Tired and tested tips on where to find further information

References

Darby, D., & Walsh, K. (2005). *Neuropsychology. A clinical approach* (5th ed.). Elsevier.

Delis, D. C., Kramer, J. H., Kaplan, E., & Ober, B. A. (2017). *Manual for the California verbal learning test, 3rd edition (CVLT-III)*. The Psychological Corporation.

Delis, D. C., Kramer, J. H., Kaplan, E., & Ober, B. A. (1994). *Manual for the California verbal learning test children's version*. The Psychological Corporation.

Folstein, M. F., Folstein, S. E., & McHugh, P. R. (1975). "Mini-Mental-State". A practical method for grading the cognitive state for clinician. *Journal of Psychiatric Research, 12*, 189–198.

Forsyth, R., & Newton, R. (2018). *Oxford specialist handbooks in paediatrics – Paediatric neurology*. University Press.

Hein, C. (2017). *Patientenstudie zu Veränderungen kognitiver und affektiver Parameter bei Patienten mit schwerem amnestischen Syndrom unterschiedlicher Ätiologie in der Rehabilitation Eine empirische Studie mit einer besonderen Patientengruppe*. Masterarbeit an der Fernuniversität Hagen.

Hildebrandt, H. (2019). *Cognitive rehabilitation of memory*. Academic.

Hacke, W. (2016). *Neurologie* (14. Aufl.). Springer.

Huggenberger, S., Moser, N., Schröder, H., Cozzi, B., Granato, A., & Merighi, A. (2019). *Neuroanatomie des Menschen*. Springer.

Kitwood, T., & Bredin, K. (1992). Towards a theory of dementia care: Personhood and well-being. *Ageing and Society, 12*(3), 269–287. https://doi.org/10.1017/S0144686X0000502X

Kalbe, E., Calabrese, P., Kohn, N., Hilker, R., Riedel, O., Wittchen, H., Dodel, R., Otto, J., Ebersbach, G., & Kessler, J. (2008). Screening for cognitive deficits in Parkinson's disease with the Parkinson neuropsychometric dementia assessment (PANDA) Instrument. *Parkinsonism & Related Disorders, 14*, S.93–S101. https://doi.org/10.1016/j.parkreldis.2007.06.008

Kolb, B., & Wishaw, I. (2021). *Fundamentals of human neuropsychology* (8th ed.). Worth.

Lezak, M., Howieson, D., Bigler, E., & Tranel, D. (2012). *Neuropsychological assessment* (5th ed.). Oxford University Press.

Maier, M., Ballester, B. R., & Verschure, P. (2019). Principles of neurorehabilitation after stroke based on motor learning and brain plasticity mechanisms. *Frontiers in Systems Neuroscience, 13.* https://doi.org/10.3389/fnsys.2019.00074

Manji, H., Connolly, S., Kitchen, N., Lambert, C., & Mehta, A. (2014). *Oxford handbook of neurology* (Oxford Medical Handbooks) (2nd ed.). University Press.

Melby-Lervåg, M., Redick, T. S., & Hulme, C. (2016). Working memory training does not improve performance on measures of intelligence or other measures of "far transfer": evidence from a meta-analytic review. *Perspectives on Psychological Science: A Journal of the Association for Psychological Science, 11*(4), 512–534. https://doi.org/10.1177/1745691616635612

Meyers, J., & Meyers, K. (1996). *Rey complex figure and the recognition trial. Professional manual. Supplemental norms for children and adolescents.* Psychological Assessment Resources.

Nasreddine, Z., Phillips, N., & Bedirian, V. (2005). The Montreal Cognitive Assessment, MoCA: A brief screening tool for mild cognitive impairment. *Journal of the American Geriatrics Society, 53,* 695–699.

Prigatano, G. (1999). *Principles of neuropsychological rehabilitation.* University Press.

Ravdin, L. D., & Katzen, H. L. (2019). *Handbook on the neuropsychology of aging and dementia* (Clinical handbooks in neuropsychology). Springer.

Scholz, A., & Niepel, A. (2019). *Das CC©-Konzept.* Hogrefe.

Strauss, E., Sherman, E., & Spreen, O. (2006). *A compendium of neuropsychological tests* (3rd ed.). Oxford University Press.

Thoma, P., Friedmann, C., & Suchan, B. (2013). Empathy and social problem solving in alcohol dependence, mood disorders and selected personality disorders. *Neuroscience and Biobehavioral Reviews, 37*(2013), 448–470.

Trapp, W., Heid, A., Röder, S., Wimmer, F., & Hajak, G. (2022). Cognitive remediation in psychiatric disorders: State of the evidence, future perspectives, and some bold ideas. *Brain Sciences, 12,* 683. https://doi.org/10.3390/brainsci12060683

Wechsler, D. (2009). *The Wechsler Memory Scale-4th edition (WMS-IV).* Pearson Assessments.

Wechsler, D. (2010). *The Wechsler Adult Intelligence Scale – 4th edition (WAIS-IV).* Pearson Assessments.

Wilson, B., Greenfield, E., Clare, L., Baddeley, A., Cockburn, J., Watson, P., Tate, R., Sopena, S., & Nannery, R. (2008). *Rivermead behavioural memory test* (3rd ed.). Pearson Assessment.

Winson, R., Wilson, B., & Bateman, A. (2017). *The brain injury rehabilitation workbook.* Guilford Press.

Printed in the United States
by Baker & Taylor Publisher Services